Understanding
the Human Body

Understanding
the Senses

Carol Ballard

rosen publishing's
rosen central®

New York

Published in 2010 by The Rosen Publishing Group Inc.
29 East 21st Street, New York, NY 10010

First Edition

Library of Congress Cataloging-in-Publication Data

Ballard, Carol.
 Understanding the senses / Carol Ballard. -- 1st ed.
      p. cm. --   (Understanding the human body)
 Includes index.
 ISBN 978-1-4358-9683-3 (library binding)
 ISBN 978-1-4358-9689-5 (paperback)
 ISBN 978-1-4358-9698-7 (6-pack)
 1. Senses and sensation--Juvenile literature. I. Title.
 QP434.B357 2010
 612.8--dc22

                          2009028249

Photo Credits:
Istockphoto.com: p. 11 (Tim Mainero), p. 13 (Tony Tremblay), p. 15 (Ben Blankenburg),
p. 22 (David Gunn), p. 23 (Christian Lagereek), p. 28 (Stefan Klein), pp. 29 (TommL),
p. 30 (Kirby Hamilton), pp. 35 (forestpath), p. 39 (Diego Cervo); Science Photo
Library: p. 20 (Steve Gschmeissner), p. 33 (Prof. P.Motta/Dept of Anatomy/
University "La Sapienza," Rome), p. 36 (Anatomical Travelogue);
Shutterstock: cover and p. 24 (Petrenko Andriy), title page and p. 8
(Constant), p. 6 (Konstantin Sutyagin), p. 7 (Ian Scott), p. 9 (Kevin Lepp),
p. 17 (Jamalludin), p. 19 (Karin Lau), p. 27 (Liudmila P. Sundikora), p. 37
(Yuri Arcurs), p. 38 (Ricardo Verde Costa), p. 40 (Stanislav Mikhalev),
p. 41 (Mike Pluth); U. S. Customs and Border Protection: p. 26
(James Tourtellotte)

Manufactured in China
CPSIA Compliance Information: Batch #WAW0102YA: For Further Information contact
Rosen Publishing, New York, New York at 1-800-237-9932

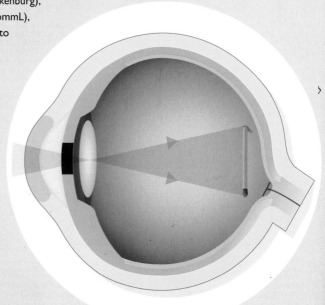

Contents

Connecting with the world

Humans have five senses: sight, hearing, smell, taste, and touch. It is through these senses that we interact with the world around us. Without our senses, life would be dangerous. For example, we would not hear fire alarms or see red traffic lights. Life would also be very dull and isolated. We would have no idea what was around us, and we would not be able to communicate with other people.

Sensory equipment

The parts of the body that are involved in our ability to sense things are the brain, nerves, and sense organs, such as the eyes and ears. These are all part of the nervous system. The intricate network of nerves links the brain to every part of the body, enabling it to receive and send signals to coordinate every function and process that occurs.

Signals to the brain

Sense organs act as a link between the brain and the world outside. When something stimulates a sense organ, it reacts by sending a signal.

This signal travels from the sense organ to the brain via the nerves. The brain interprets it and we understand what stimulated the sense organ. This might sound like a long process, but it all happens in the tiniest fraction of a second.

The part of the brain involved with the senses is called the cerebral cortex. This is also the part where our thinking processes are carried out. Different areas of the cerebral cortex are associated with different senses. For instance, sight is associated with an area at the back of the cerebral cortex, hearing with a low central area, and taste with an area just above the hearing area.

Our senses can help to protect us and keep us safe. The flashing lights and screeching sirens from this ambulance alert our eyes and ears to its speed and direction.

Sharks such as the one in this picture can detect electric currents in the water around them. This can help them to locate their prey, and also to navigate.

Sensory problems

In some people, one or more senses may not work as well as in other people. Lack of sight or hearing can have a profound effect on many aspects of everyday life, but an impaired sense of smell, taste, or touch generally causes far fewer problems.

There are many different causes of impaired senses, and many ways of overcoming the difficulties that such disabilities present. For example, some blind or partially sighted people use the Braille system to read and write. This system uses patterns of raised dots to represent characters that can be read through touch. Also, hearing aids can help many people with hearing difficulties.

 Investigate

Humans have only five senses, but some other creatures can sense things that we cannot. Find out about some of these extra senses, the creatures that have them, and the sense organs that they use. You could begin by finding out about:

• how fish and some amphibians sense water currents and water pressure

• how pit vipers sense the heat given off by other creatures

Looking at eyes

We all know what eyes look like, but have you ever looked very closely at them? An eye is made up of several individually named parts. Each part of the eye, and the structures around it, has its own special function. Some of these are involved in vision, and others protect the eye.

Eye sockets

Our eyes are protected by the skull bones. Each eye lies in a bony ring called the orbit, or eye socket, and is held in place by delicate muscles and tough bands called ligaments. The muscles also move the eyes within the sockets.

Eyebrows and eyelids

The eyebrows are rows of hairs above each eye. These protect the eyes by keeping dust and dirt away from them. They also stop moisture, such as sweat and rain, from trickling down into the eyes.

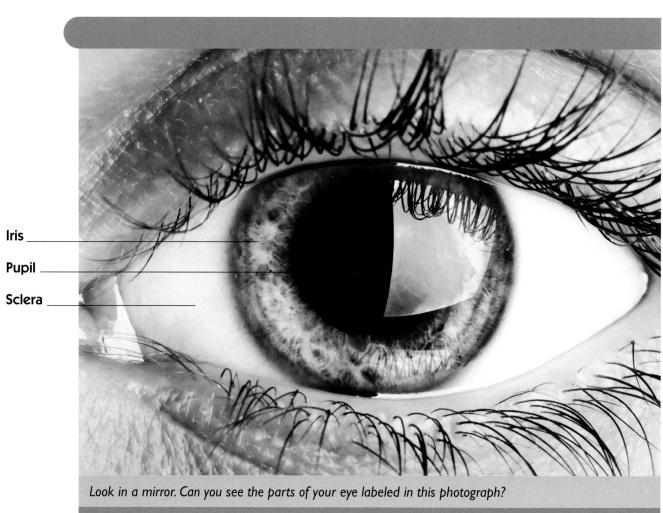

Iris _____

Pupil _____

Sclera _____

Look in a mirror. Can you see the parts of your eye labeled in this photograph?

The eyelids are folds of skin above and below each eye. Rows of eyelash hairs along the edges of the upper and lower eyelids prevent dust and dirt from entering the eye. The eyelids shut regularly, spreading a lubricating fluid across the surface of the eyes.

Pupil and cornea

At the center of each eye is a black dot. This is actually a tiny hole called the pupil, and it is covered by a transparent layer called the cornea. Light passes through the cornea and enters the eye through the pupil.

Iris and sclera

The colored ring around the pupil is called the iris. The overall color of your iris is inherited from your parents. The iris is not a single, solid color, though—it is patterned with lighter and darker areas. Amazingly, no two people have identical iris patterns.

The white area that makes up the rest of the front of the eye is called the sclera. It is a tough membrane that helps to give the eye its shape.

Conjunctiva

The conjunctiva is a thin, transparent membrane that covers the surface of the eyeball and the inner surfaces of the eyelids. It is slightly slack at the edges to allow the eyeball to move.

Reacting to light

The iris is made of rings of muscle that control the amount of light entering the eye. In dim light, the outer ring of iris muscles contracts.

Tears are produced in the tear glands under the upper eyelids. Tears help to keep the eyes clean and moist.

This pulls the iris toward its outer edge, making the pupil bigger so that more light can enter the eye. In bright light, the inner ring of iris muscles contracts. This pulls the iris toward its center, making the pupil smaller so that less light enters the eye.

How do we see?

The sense of sight is called vision. Light sources such as the Sun, light bulbs, and candles, give out light energy. This travels away from the light source in straight lines. You can sometimes see straight shafts of sunlight shining through a gap between clouds. When the light reaches solid objects, it bounces off of them. If some of the scattered light enters our eyes, we "see" the object.

Process of seeing

Seeing an object is not a single event, however. There are several steps in the process. First, light rays bounce off of the object and onto the transparent cornea. As they pass through the cornea, the light rays are bent a little. The light rays travel through a watery liquid called the aqueous humor.

The light rays then pass through the pupil to the lens. This is a jellylike disk that bends the light rays even more as they pass through it. As the light rays continue travelling, they pass through the center of the eye, which is filled with a gel called vitreous humor.

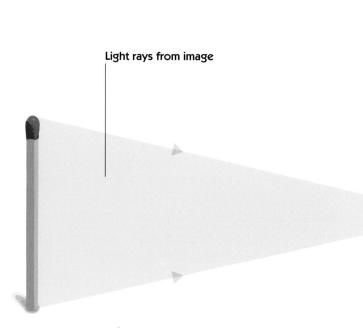

Light rays from image

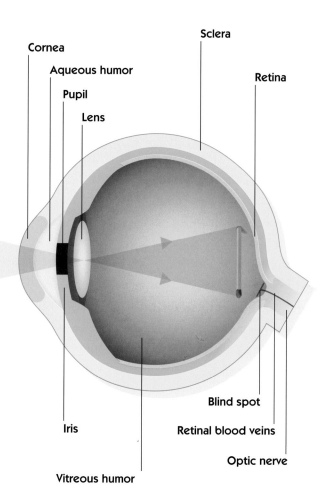

Cornea

Aqueous humor

Pupil

Lens

Sclera

Retina

Blind spot

Retinal blood veins

Optic nerve

Iris

Vitreous humor

▲ *This diagram shows how light rays from an object enter the eye. An upside-down image is focused on the retina.*

At the back of the eye is a light-sensitive membrane called the retina. When the light rays stimulate the retina, it responds by sending electrical signals to the brain via the optic nerve. The area of the retina where the optic nerve joins it is not light sensitive. This is called the "blind spot."

Finally, the vision center in the brain receives the signals from the optic nerve. It interprets the information and we "see" the object.

Seeing solids

When we look at something, we see a solid, three-dimensional object and are able to judge how far away it is. This is because each eye has a slightly different view and sends a slightly different signal to the brain. The brain then interprets the two signals and works out the three-dimensional shape and also how far away it is.

Peripheral vision

When we look straight ahead, we see whatever is in front of us. Our eyes also receive light rays from each side. This is called "peripheral vision." Most people have a field of vision of about 100 degrees on each side, making a total field of vision of about 200 degrees.

Detecting movement at the sides can be important when playing some sports, because it enables a player to catch a glimpse of a ball or opponent a long way to his side. It is also important to drivers, making them aware of vehicles and pedestrians that are not immediately in front of them.

Try this

This activity shows that you really do have a blind spot! Close your left eye and look at the cross below. Slowly move the book toward your face. You will find that, at some point, the image of the dot will disappear. This is the point at which the image of the dot lands on the blind spot. Try it again, this time with your right eye covered and your left eye looking at the dot.

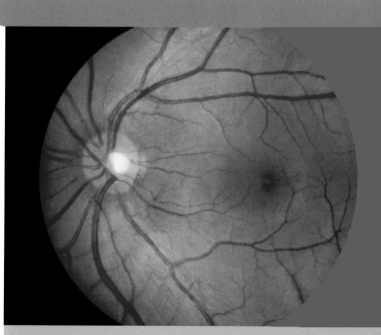

This close-up view of a healthy retina is taken using an instrument called an ophthalmoscope. The bright area is the blind spot, at the junction of the retina and the optic nerve.

Color vision

Most people can see a full range of colors. They are able to do so because some specialized cells in the retina are color-sensitive. This means that the cells are stimulated and respond when light of a particular color reaches them.

The retina is the light-sensitive layer at the back of the eye. It contains nerve cells called neurons and light-sensitive cells that are called photoreceptors. There are two types of photoreceptor: rods and cones.

Rods

Rods are long, thin cells and they allow us to see in very dim light. They contain a light-absorbing chemical called rhodopsin, which is sensitive to low light intensities. Each retina contains about 120 million rods.

Cones

Cones are shorter and fatter than rods, and their tips are cone-shaped. They need stronger light intensities than rods to work. There are three different types of cone, each containing a different light-absorbing chemical. One type is sensitive to red light, one type to blue light, and one type to green light.

The brain works out the color of what we are looking at from the different numbers of each cone type that are stimulated. For instance, looking at a red flower will stimulate mainly

▼ *This diagram shows what happens when light falls on the retina and stimulates rods and cones. Signals are sent from the rods and cones to the brain via the optic nerve.*

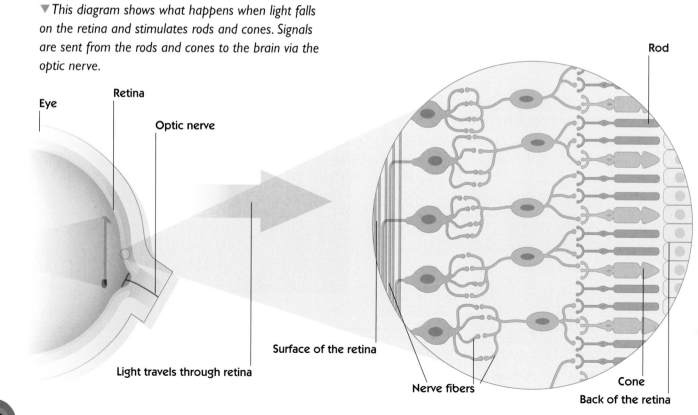

Eye

Retina

Optic nerve

Rod

Light travels through retina

Surface of the retina

Nerve fibers

Cone

Back of the retina

Color-blindness is an inherited condition, which means it is passed from one generation to the next. Because it is a gender-linked condition, color-blindness is much more common in men than in women. Find out how gender-linked inheritance works, and its role in color-blindness.

red cones, and looking at green leaves will stimulate mainly green cones. Each retina contains about 6.5 million cones.

Color-blindness

Some people are color-blind. This means they cannot distinguish between some colors. The most common type of color-blindness is red-green, which means a person cannot tell the difference between red and green. A rarer type of color-blindness prevents people from distinguishing between blue and yellow.

Testing for color-blindness

Special test cards, called Ishihara cards, are used to test for color-blindness. They are covered with dots of varying sizes and shades. People with normal vision are able to distinguish numbers within the patterns. People who are color-blind just see random dot patterns.

Living with color-blindness

Although being color-blind may not seem like a serious problem, it can cause some difficulties. For instance, how would you tell whether a

A person with normal vision would see the picture on the left. A person with red-green color-blindness would see the duller picture on the right.

traffic light was showing red or green if you were red-green color-blind? How would you know which color ball you were aiming at on a pool table? Some jobs, such as that of an airline pilot, rely on a person being able to distinguish between colors and are not open to color-blind people. This is usually for the protection and safety of both the color-blind person and others.

Eyesight problems

Although many people have excellent eyesight, some find it difficult to see things that are close to them and others find it hard to see things in the distance. Some people have other problems with their vision. Glasses, contact lenses, and surgery can overcome many of the problems.

Being nearsighted

Nearsightedness is called myopia, and people who are nearsighted are said to be myopic. They may be able to see things close to them, but distant objects look fuzzy or blurred. It happens because the light rays focus in front of, instead of on, the retina. Then the image that forms on the retina is indistinct.

Nearsightedness can be caused by the lens being too strong or the eyeball being too long. It can be corrected by a concave (inwardly curved) lens. This spreads the light rays out before they reach the lens, so that they focus perfectly on the retina.

▼ *In the top diagram, the light rays are focused in front of the retina in a nearsighted person. Below, the lens corrects this and the image is focused on the retina.*

Being farsighted

Farsightedness is the opposite of nearsightedness. It is called hyperopia, and people who are farsighted are said to be hyperopic. They may be able to see things in the distance, but objects close to them look fuzzy or blurred. This is because the light rays focus behind the retina, so the image that forms on the retina is indistinct.

Farsightedness can be caused by the lens being too weak or the eyeball being too short. It can be corrected by a convex (outwardly curved) lens. This bends light rays inward before they reach the lens, so that they focus perfectly on the retina.

▼ *In the top diagram, the light rays are focused behind the retina in a farsighted person. Below, the lens corrects this and the image is focused on the retina.*

Light rays focus in front of retina

Myopia (nearsightedness)

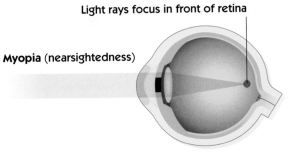

Light rays focus behind retina

Hypermetropia (farsightedness)

Light rays focus on retina

Myopia corrected with concave lens

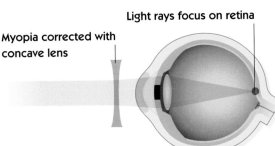

Light rays focus on retina

Hypermetropia corrected with convex lens

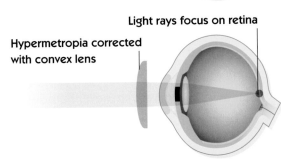

Laser surgery

In recent years, laser surgery has become increasingly common for the correction of nearsightedness and farsightedness. A laser beam is used to alter the shape of the cornea, so that light focuses correctly on the retina. For many people, this can mean that they no longer need to wear spectacles or contact lenses.

Astigmatism

Astigmatism means that the curved surface of the cornea or lens is uneven. It causes a blurred and distorted view of everything. Using lenses that bend light more in one direction than in another can correct most cases of astigmatism.

Cataracts

Cataracts are a common cause of blindness, especially among the elderly and in people with some illnesses and conditions such as diabetes. Instead of being clear, the lens becomes increasingly cloudy until eventually it is opaque. This means that no light can pass through it and so the person is unable to see. Removing the damaged lens by surgery and replacing it with a plastic lens can restore the person's sight.

Taking care of your eyes

Eyes are delicate and so they need to be taken care of. Exposure to very bright light can cause long-term damage, so it makes sense to wear sunglasses on sunny days. Dark glasses or goggles are important when skiing, too, because sunlight reflected by white snow can be dazzling. It is also advisable to have an eye test every two years. This can help to detect eye diseases in the early stages.

Body facts

Spectacles may seem like a modern invention, but people have used lenses to help correct defective eyesight for hundreds of years.

- An Italian monk mentioned "eyeglasses" in a letter he wrote in 1306 and said they had been invented 20 years before that date!

- The first eyeglasses had no arms and just perched on the bridge of the nose.

The dark glasses these skiers are wearing will protect their eyes from the glare of sunlight on the snow.

Looking at ears

We often refer to the flaps at each side of the head as our "ears." However, these are only a small part of each ear—the rest is buried inside the skull. This means that the delicate structures that allow us to hear are protected by the strong bones around them. The ear has three main parts: the outer ear, the middle ear, and the inner ear.

Outer ear

The pinna is the flap of skin and cartilage at the side of the head. The lower edge of the pinna is called the lobe. It can either slope upward or dip down and then up. Lobe shape is inherited in the same way as eye color. The pinna acts as a funnel for sound waves, and leads to a bony tube called the ear canal. The inner end of the ear canal is blocked by a thin membrane that is stretched across it. This is the eardrum, or tympanic membrane.

Middle ear

The space beyond the outer ear is the middle ear. It is a small space containing a chain of three tiny bones called the ossicles. Individually, these each have a name based on its shape: the hammer, anvil, and stirrup. Each is held in place by minute muscles and strong bands called ligaments.

At the inner side of the middle ear is a membrane called the oval window. Leading out of the middle ear is the eustachian tube, which is sometimes called the auditory tube. This links the middle ear and the upper part of the throat.

Inner ear

This is the innermost part of the ear. It contains the cochlea, which is a complex maze of spaces curled around in a spiral of bone. At the base of the cochlea is a membrane called the round window, which leads to the middle ear. The cochlea is linked to the auditory nerve, which carries signals from the cochlea to the brain. Structures called semicircular canals, which are involved in balance, also lie in the inner ear.

▶ The diagram shows a sound wave traveling through the air to the ear. You can also see the organization of the structures that make up the outer ear, middle ear, and inner ear.

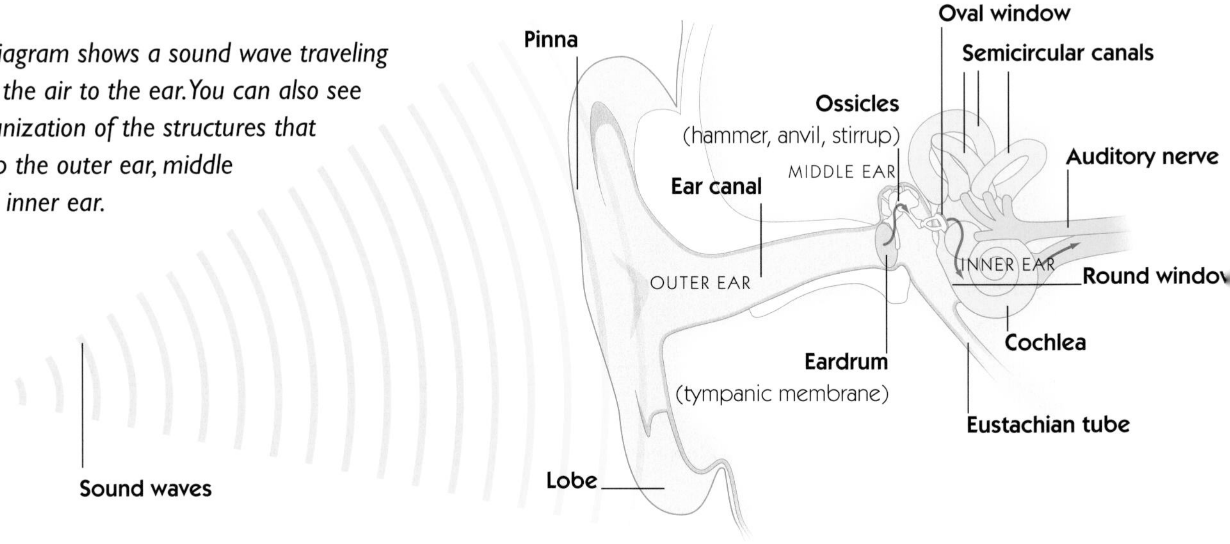

Pinna

Oval window

Semicircular canals

Ossicles
(hammer, anvil, stirrup)

MIDDLE EAR

Auditory nerve

Ear canal

OUTER EAR

INNER EAR

Round window

Eardrum
(tympanic membrane)

Cochlea

Eustachian tube

Sound waves

Lobe

Balance

The three fluid-filled, semicircular canals in the inner ear are arranged at right-angles to each other, like the front, side, and bottom of a box. Underneath them are two sacs called the utricle and saccule. Each sac contains sensory hair cells in a gel-like substance. Together, the semicircular canals, utricle, and saccule are called the vestibular apparatus. They detect movements of your head and control your balance.

Investigate

Have you ever been to an amusement park and felt sick or dizzy as you whirl around on a ride? Or perhaps felt sick with the motion of a car, bus, or boat? These feelings are all to do with your eyes and ears sending your brain conflicting signals. Find out more about motion sickness and why it happens.

Whirling around on a fairground ride like this can make some people feel dizzy and sick!

How do we hear?

The term auditory refers to the sense of hearing. Sound sources, such as people's voices, musical instruments, and machinery, vibrate to make sounds. These vibrations travel through the air as waves. When sound waves travel from a sound source to our ears, we "hear" the sound.

Process of hearing

Several steps are involved in the hearing process. It begins when sound waves travel from a sound source through the air. They reach the pinna, which acts as a funnel, directing the waves in toward the ear canal. The sound waves travel along the ear canal toward the eardrum.

When the sound waves reach the eardrum, they make it vibrate. These vibrations of the eardrum cause the hammer to vibrate. This then makes the anvil vibrate, which in turn makes the stirrup vibrate.

These stirrup vibrations make the oval window vibrate. Vibrations then pass from the oval window into the fluid that fills the cochlea. Here, the vibrations in the fluid make some of the tiny hair cells bend. These send signals to the brain via the auditory nerve. The brain interprets the signals and then you "hear" the sound.

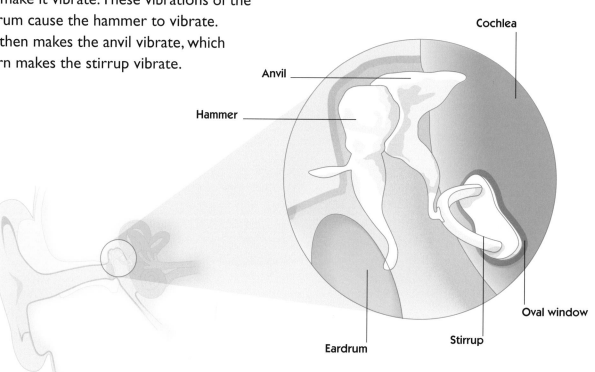

Anvil
Hammer
Cochlea
Oval window
Stirrup
Eardrum

▲ Here, you can see how the three tiny ossicles of the middle ear are arranged. The hammer is linked to the eardrum and the stirrup is linked to the oval window, the opening leading to the inner ear. The anvil is linked to the two other bones.

The vibrations in the cochlear fluid continue all the way around the spiral. Eventually, they pass from the cochlea to the round window, and out into the middle ear, where they dissipate, or cease to exist.

Pinpointing sounds

Some animals can move their pinnae to help them accurately pinpoint the direction of a sound. Humans cannot do this, but we can tell the general direction from which a sound comes.

As sound waves travel, they will reach one ear a fraction of a second before the other. This means that the signal from the ear closest to the sound source will reach the brain a tiny fraction of a second before the signal from the

Body facts

The ossicles are the tiniest bones in the body. The stirrup, which is the smallest, is only 0.1–0.14 inch (2.5–3.5 millimeters) long! Amazingly, these three strangely-shaped bones are vital to your sense of hearing, even though they are so small.

other ear. Also, the sound will be louder in the ear closest to the sound source. The brain uses these differences in timing and volume to work out where the sound is coming from.

▼ *Here, the sound is coming from the man's left. The sound vibrations reach his left ear a fraction of a second before they reach his right ear, allowing the brain to work out which direction the sound is coming from.*

Sound waves

Hearing different sounds

There are many different types of sound. High-pitched whistles, low-pitched rumbles of traffic, loud shouts, and quiet whispers are all audible to us. Because our hearing mechanism is complex, we are able to distinguish these differences in sound.

Pitch

Pitch is a measure of how high or low a sound is, and is measured in units called hertz (Hz). For instance, a whistle makes a high-pitched sound and a bass drum makes a low-pitched sound. Sound waves of high-pitched sounds have fast vibrations. They are detected by the part of the cochlea nearest the oval window.

Sound waves of low-pitched sounds have slow vibrations. They are detected by the innermost part of the cochlea. Only the part of the cochlea that detects the sound sends a signal to the brain. The brain knows which part of the cochlea the signal has come from, and so it is able to work out the pitch of the sound.

Loud or soft sound

Volume is a measure of how loud or soft a sound is, and is measured in units called decibels (dB). The louder the sound, the bigger the vibrations of the sound wave will be. The bigger the vibrations, the more hair cells they will stimulate. Only those hair cells that are stimulated send signals to the brain. The brain works out the volume of the sound from the number of hair cells that send it signals.

Limits of human hearing

Human ears cannot detect every sound that is made. Some are too high, too low, or too quiet. Others are so loud that they damage the ears.

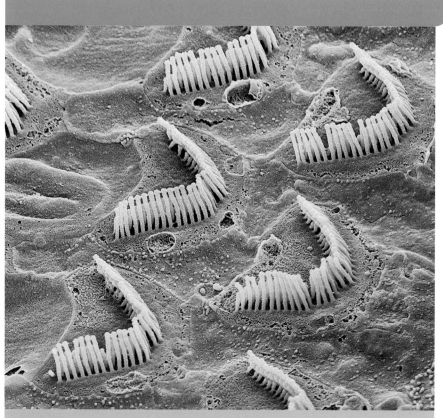

This photograph, taken using a microscope, shows the tiny hairs that respond to vibrations by sending signals to the brain via the auditory nerve.

Pitch limits Most adults with normal hearing can detect sounds in the range 30 to 20,000 Hz. Human ears are most responsive to sounds in the range 300 to 3000 Hz. This is approximately the range made by the human voice.

Volume limits The volume of 0 dB is called the threshold of human hearing. A person with normal hearing cannot detect sounds quieter than this. The volume of 130 dB is called the threshold of pain, and sounds louder than this damage the ears. Everyday sounds such as normal conversation are roughly 50–70 dB.

Investigate

Some animals can hear sounds outside the range of pitches detected by most humans. For instance, bats can detect sounds in the range 2,000–110,000 Hz. Elephants can detect sounds that are too low for a human to hear. Their hearing range is 16–12,000 Hz. Find out more about the sense of hearing in different animals.

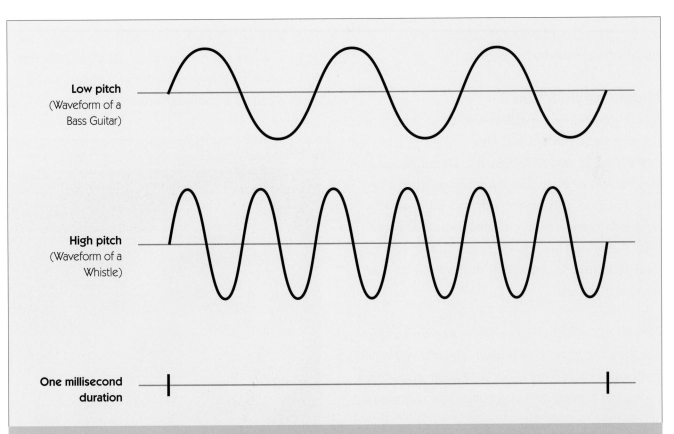

Low pitch
(Waveform of a
Bass Guitar)

High pitch
(Waveform of a
Whistle)

One millisecond
duration

The bottom line shows a scale of one millisecond. The middle line shows the pattern of a high-pitched sound wave. The top line shows the pattern of a low-pitched sound wave. You can see that the high-pitched sound has more wave peaks in a millisecond than the low-pitched sound.

Problems with hearing

Some people cannot hear as well as others. Depending on the cause, this may be a temporary or permanent condition. In some cases, the hearing loss is so small that the person is hardly aware of it. In others, though, the hearing loss can be so great that it seriously affects a person's life.

Ear infections

Infection of the middle ear is known as otitis media. It often follows a cold or sore throat, as bacteria reach the middle ear via the eustachian tube. Pus fills the middle ear, raising the pressure and pushing against the eardrum, which becomes red and bulges outward. Hearing is impaired and it may sound as if there are ringing noises inside the head. Middle ear infections can usually be treated with antibiotics.

Middle ear infection

In severe middle ear infections, thick fluid builds up inside the middle ear, preventing the ossicles vibrating and reducing hearing. Decongestant medicine may clear the fluid. Sometimes, a tiny hole is made in the eardrum and the fluid is drained. A small, plastic drainage tube is fitted into the hole. This lets air reach the middle ear. The grommet is eventually pushed out as the eardrum grows.

Middle ear infections can affect people of any age, but are most common in children younger than eight years. This is because their eustachian tubes are smaller and so get blocked more easily.

Aging and hearing

Most people suffer some degree of hearing loss as they get older. In many cases, normal hearing can be achieved by wearing a hearing aid.

Lots of different types are available, and modern digital models provide a highly sophisticated level of control, allowing the wearer to adjust the device to suit different environments by a single click of a button.

Deafness

Some medical conditions can result in hearing loss. In many cases, hearing aids can overcome the problem. Patients whose cochlea does not function properly may undergo surgery to fit a device called a cochlear implant.

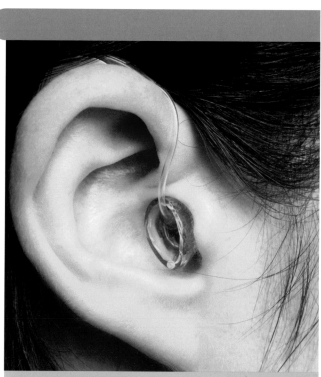

This is a modern hearing aid, in place in a girl's ear. Being very small, and made of transparent plastic, it is very discreet.

These men work in a very noisy environment, so they safeguard their ears by wearing ear protectors with efficient insulation. These are made of materials that sound waves cannot travel through.

Hearing loss cannot always be remedied. People who suffer from permanent deafness may use lip reading and sign language to communicate. Hearing dogs can alert them to sounds such as doorbells and fire alarms, and modern technology such as videophones can also be helpful.

Take care of your ears

Many people enjoy listening to music via devices such as MP3 players with headphones. At low volumes, this is fine. If the sound is turned up too far, though, the ears may suffer long-term damage. As a general guide, if somebody else near you can hear your music when you have your headphones in, you need to turn the volume down.

Try this

You can protect your ears from loud noises by wearing ear protectors. These work because the sound waves cannot travel through them as easily as they can travel through air. The materials they are made from are good sound insulators. Try making pads of different materials such as absorbent cotton, blanket, tinfoil, or cardboard. Hold one close to your ears and ask a friend to make a loud noise. Test each pad. Are some materials better sound insulators than others?

Inside the nose

Our sense of smell allows us to enjoy a variety of pleasant things such as the scent of flowers or the smell of a delicious meal. It can also warn us of danger. For instance, food that is not fit to eat often smells unpleasant and so we avoid eating it. But how does your nose detect the smells around you?

Nasal cavity

The nose has two separate holes called nostrils. The nostrils are lined with hairs that filter out dust and other particles from the air. Both nostrils lead to a single hollow space behind the face called the nasal cavity, and it is here that smells are detected.

Mucus

The roof of the nasal cavity is covered with a layer of thick fluid called mucus. This is produced by olfactory glands in the lining layer of the nasal cavity, and is carried to the surface of the nasal cavity by ducts. The mucus keeps the surface of the nasal cavity moist. Chemicals that enter the nasal cavity dissolve in the mucus. This is important because the receptor cells are covered by the mucus and can only detect chemicals that are dissolved in it.

Receptor cells

The lining of the roof of the nasal cavity is called the olfactory (or nasal) epithelium. It contains millions of special cells called olfactory receptor cells. Tiny, hairlike fibers called cilia hang down from the receptor cells into the nasal cavity.

The receptor cells only live for about one month, so they are continually replaced with new cells. These develop from basal stem cells that lie among the receptor cells.

Using her sense of smell, this girl is able to enjoy the scent of fresh flowers.

Between the receptor cells and the basal stem cells are supporting cells. These are simple cells whose function is to support the receptor cells and basal stem cells.

The receptor cells are linked to an area called the olfactory bulb. You have two of these bulblike structures located at the base of the brain, above the nasal cavity. The olfactory bulb in turn is linked to the olfactory nerves, which carry signals from the receptor cells to the brain.

Body facts

Most adult humans can distinguish between about 10,000 different smells, and there are more than 20 million receptor cells in a human nasal epithelium. Some dogs may have one hundred times this number—so imagine how sensitive their sense of smell must be!

▼ *This diagram shows the structures that respond to smells and the route taken by signals sent from the nose to the brain.*

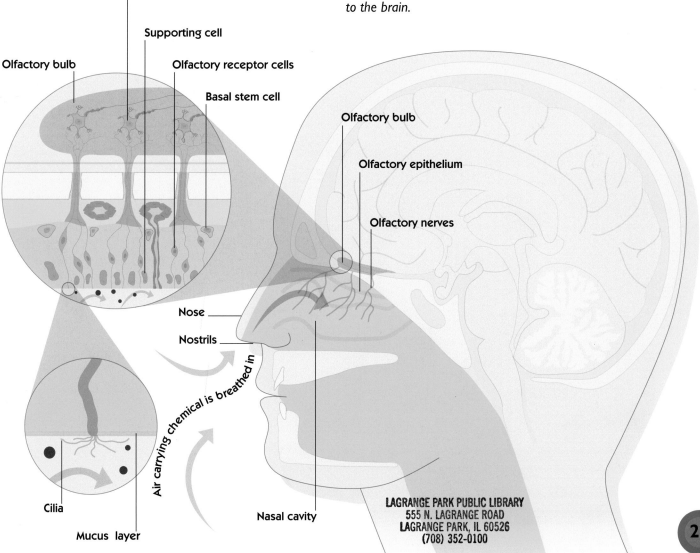

Olfactory nerve cell

Supporting cell

Olfactory bulb

Olfactory receptor cells

Basal stem cell

Olfactory bulb

Olfactory epithelium

Olfactory nerves

Nose

Nostrils

Air carrying chemical is breathed in

Cilia

Mucus layer

Nasal cavity

How do we smell?

The medical term for the sense of smell is olfaction. The nose is part of the respiratory system, allowing air to enter our bodies. As we breathe in, chemicals in the air enter the nose and we "smell" them.

The process of smelling

When a chemical is released into the air and gradually spreads around the process of smelling begins. The air containing the chemical is drawn into the nasal cavity when you breathe in. Inside the nasal cavity, the chemical dissolves in the layer of mucus covering the nasal epithelium.

The receptor cells of the nasal epithelium detect the chemical in the mucus. These receptor cells then react by sending a signal to the brain. This signal travels via the olfactory nerves. When the brain receives the signal, it interprets the information. It is at this point that we "smell" the chemical.

Many dogs have a much keener sense of smell than humans. Some, like this sniffer dog working at an airport, can be trained to detect minute amounts of substances such as drugs and explosives.

Try this

What can you smell? Ask a friend to put small amounts of a variety of different foods on separate dishes. These could be foods such as salt, sugar, orange juice, coffee, garlic, and chocolate. Then put on a blindfold and ask your friend to hold the dishes, one at a time, at arm's length from your nose. Can you detect what food is in the dish? If not, ask your friend to move the dish closer to your nose. If you still cannot smell anything, try sniffing. Which food did you get right at a distance? Which did you need to sniff? Were there any foods that you could not smell at all?

Spraying perfume from a bottle releases chemicals into the air. We breathe them in, and when they have dissolved in the mucus of the nasal epithelium, we smell the perfume.

What we can't smell

Our sense of smell is not perfect, because we can only smell chemicals that are a) released into the air and b) can dissolve in the mucus. For instance, you may be able to see a liquid perfume inside a glass bottle, but you cannot tell what it smells like until you take the lid off the bottle or spray some into the air.

Unfortunately, there are some dangerous chemicals that we cannot smell, such as carbon monoxide and natural gas. Carbon monoxide may be given off by equipment such as faulty heaters. Special detectors are available that make a loud noise if the level of carbon monoxide rises above a normal level. To alert us if there is a natural gas leak, one or more strong-smelling chemicals are mixed with it.

Fading smells

If you walk into a room where there is a strong smell, you notice it almost immediately. After a little while, though, it will begin to seem less strong, and eventually, you may not even notice it any more. The smell has not gone away, but your nose slowly becomes less sensitive to it. This happens because your smell sensors stop sending the signals to the brain, allowing you to be aware of new smells.

Reduced sense of smell

Sometimes, we sniff at something we want to smell, drawing more air into the nasal cavity. More of the chemical that we are trying to smell is also drawn in along with the air. This means that our ability to smell the chemical is enhanced. The opposite is also true, which means that anything that reduces the amount of air entering the nose will reduce the sense of smell.

Blocked nose

When a person is suffering from a cold, their nose and sinuses (cavities within the bones of the head) often become blocked. The lining of the nasal cavity swells and extra mucus builds up. It becomes difficult for air to pass through and so the person may find it easier to breathe through the mouth rather than the nose. When this happens, the air flow through the nasal cavity is reduced and the sense of smell is impaired.

Allergies such as hay fever can also cause a blocked nose. Some medicines that reduce the swelling inside the nasal cavity and prevent the build up of mucus can reduce the problems this causes.

Damaged noses

Damage to the delicate lining of the nasal cavity may result in the reduction or total loss of the sense of smell. Smoke from cigarettes can damage the receptor cells, making them incapable of responding to chemicals. Injury from falling or

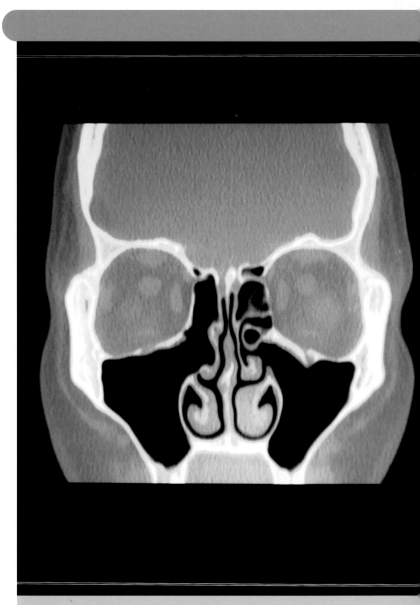

The sinuses show up as dark areas on this scan of a human head.

sports accidents may damage the olfactory nerve, which may result in the reduction or total loss of the sense of smell.

Aging

Many elderly people complain that they cannot smell as well as they could when they were younger. This is because, as people age, their olfactory receptor cells are renewed less frequently.

Smell and taste

The sense of smell also plays an important part in helping us to taste our food. This is because foods release chemicals into the air. When these enter the nose, we smell them. This provides the brain with extra information about the food and enhances the sense of taste.

Try this

Find out for yourself how much your nose helps you to distinguish between different tastes. Cut two cubes of each of a variety of foods, such as apple, carrot, cake, chocolate, and bread. Then you need to wear a blindfold and hold your nose. Ask a friend to pass you one cube on a fork. Chew it and tell your friend what you think it is. Do this for each cube one by one, and ask your friend to record each answer you give. Then repeat the process but this time without holding your nose. Did you get more right when you could smell the food as well as taste it?

The girl in this photograph has a cold, and so her nose and sinuses may be blocked, reducing her ability to taste and smell normally.

Detecting tastes

Our sense of taste allows us to distinguish between the different tastes of many foods, for instance, tangy oranges, hot chili, and sugary meringue. This is possible because there are sense organs in the mouth that are stimulated by the presence of different chemicals.

Chewing

When you want to eat, your sharp front teeth called incisors bite off a piece of food and you take it into your mouth. When you chew, your lower jaw moves up and down and the food is crushed between your strong back teeth called molars. As the food is chewed, it becomes softened. It mixes with a watery fluid known as saliva, which is made by salivary glands under the tongue and at the back of the mouth. The saliva makes the food moist and slippery.

The tongue moves the food around the mouth. It consists mainly of muscles that enable it to move in any direction, to curl around, shorten, and elongate slightly.

Taste buds

The upper surface of the tongue is rough. This is because it is covered in small bumps called papillae. These contain barrel-shaped structures called taste buds, each made up of a cluster of receptor cells. Some taste buds are present on the palate, which is the roof of the mouth. They are also found on part of the upper throat and on the flap called the epiglottis, at the back of the mouth.

Different tastes

Traditionally, four basic tastes are identified: sweet, sour, salty, and bitter. Although first described in the early twentieth century, a fifth taste called umami has only recently been added to the list. The name comes from a Japanese word that means "savory" and many people describe the taste of umami as being meaty. Scientists have found that receptor cells

Taste buds allow this boy to taste the different flavors of the tomato, pepperoni, and cheese in his pizza.

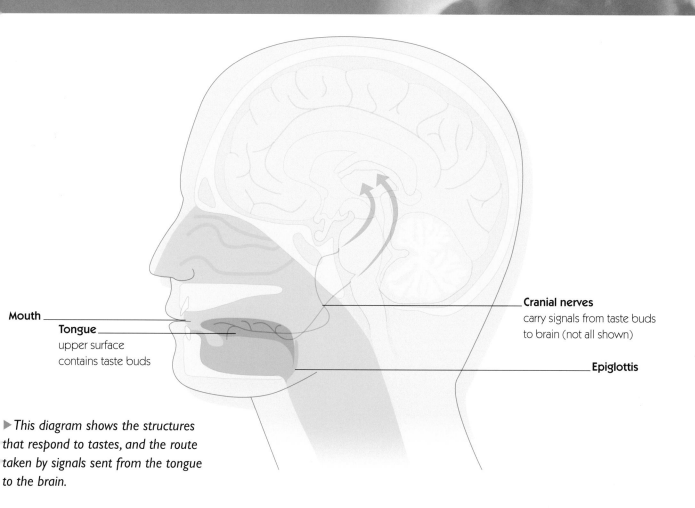

Mouth ———————————

Tongue ——————
upper surface
contains taste buds

Cranial nerves
carry signals from taste buds
to brain (not all shown)

Epiglottis

► *This diagram shows the structures
that respond to tastes, and the route
taken by signals sent from the tongue
to the brain.*

sensitive to umami respond to a chemical
called glutamate that is found in many proteins.
Recent research also suggests that there
may be receptor cells that are sensitive to
the taste of fats, and others that are sensitive
to the taste of calcium.

Five basic tastes may not seem many when you
consider the wide variety of different types of
food that we eat. The five basic tastes can be
put together in a multitude of different ways to
create the range of tastes that we enjoy in our
diet. Our perception of taste also depends on
other factors, such as the texture and the
temperature of the food.

Investigate

Some parts of the tongue are more sensitive
to one type of taste than to another. The tip
of the tongue is most sensitive to sweet
tastes and the sides to sour tastes. The tip
and front of the sides are most sensitive to
salty tastes and the back to bitter tastes.
The center of the tongue is not particularly
sensitive to any tastes. Find out more about
why we experience different tastes on
different parts of the tongue.

How do we taste?

The medical term for the sense of taste is *gustation*. When we put food into our mouths and chew, we "taste" it. The parts of our mouths that detect the taste of our food are the taste buds.

Inside a taste bud

Each taste bud is made up from about 25 receptor cells with supporting cells between them. The receptor cells only live for one to two weeks, and are continually replaced by new ones. Tiny hairlike structures extend from the tip of each receptor cell, through the opening of the taste bud, and into the surface layer of the tongue.

All the receptor cells have the same basic structure, but each has many different receptor sites for detecting different chemicals. This means that each cell can respond to a variety of different chemicals and detect a range of tastes.

Detecting a taste

Some chemicals are already dissolved in the food when they enter the mouth. Any that are not are quickly dissolved in saliva in the mouth. The hairs of the receptor cells in the taste buds detect the chemicals. The receptor cells then react by sending signals to the brain.

The signals travel to the brain via cranial nerves. Signals from the front of the tongue travel via the facial nerve. Signals from the back of the tongue travel via the glossopharyngeal nerve, and those from the palate and throat travel via the vagus nerve. When the brain receives the signals, it interprets the information and we "taste" the food.

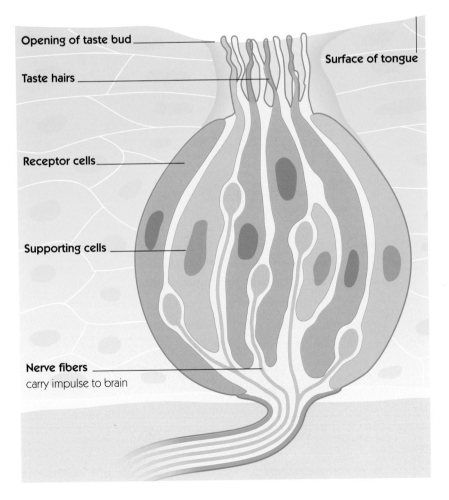

Opening of taste bud

Surface of tongue

Taste hairs

Receptor cells

Supporting cells

Nerve fibers
carry impulse to brain

◄ *Here, you can see the cells that make up a single taste bud of the tongue.*

Aging and taste

Most children have a very acute sense of taste and this may be why babies and many young children prefer relatively mild foods to hot, spicy ones. Slowly, though, our sense of taste declines as we age. This is because, the older we are, the less frequently the taste receptor cells in the taste buds are replaced. Many older people say that their food does not seem as full of flavor as it did when they were younger.

Body facts

An average tongue contains about 10,000 taste buds. Each taste bud contains about 25 receptor cells—so at a rough estimate, there will be about a quarter of a million taste receptors in your tongue.

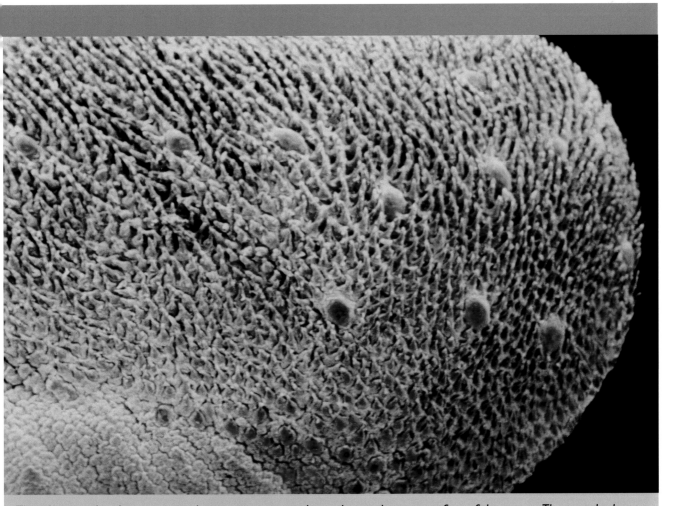

This photograph, taken using an electron microscope, shows the rough upper surface of the tongue. The taste buds are found within each of the round, pink raised areas.

Skin and touch

Our sense of touch makes us aware of things we feel, pressure, and vibrations. Special sense receptors in our skin allow us to feel these things, which are called tactile sensations. Unlike other senses, therefore, the sense of touch is located all over your body.

Inside the skin

The skin is made up of two layers. The outer layer is called the epidermis and it is made from dead cells. The cells of the epidermis are gradually worn away by our everyday activities and are continually being replaced by new cells. Some nerve endings lie in the epidermis.

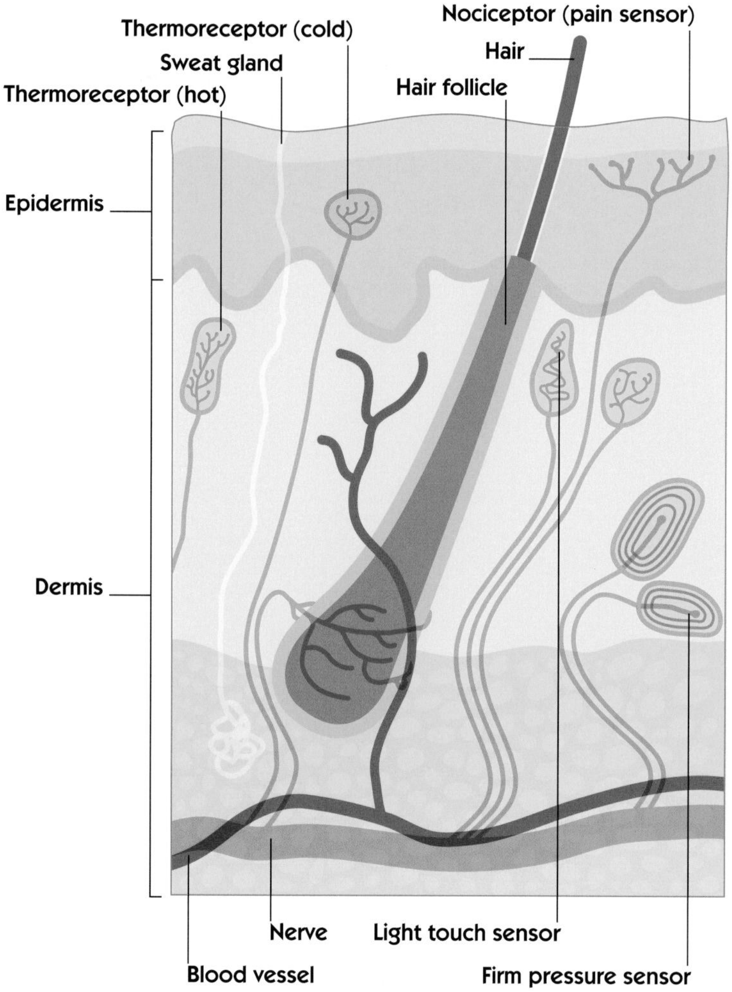

Beneath the epidermis is the inner layer of the skin, called the dermis. This contains many different structures including blood vessels, hair follicles, sweat glands, nerves, and sense receptors. Some sense receptors consist of nerve endings enclosed within an outer layer called a capsule. Other tactile sensations are detected by nerve endings that do not have a capsule. These are called free nerve endings.

Nerve signals

When nerve endings and sense receptors in the skin are stimulated, they respond by sending signals to the brain. The signals travel from the skin to the brain via the nerves. When the brain receives the information, it interprets it, and you "feel" the sensation.

Because some areas of the skin contain more sense receptors and free nerve endings than others, they are more sensitive to tactile sensations. For example, you can distinguish between different textures more easily with your fingertips than with the back of your hand.

Thermoreceptor (cold)
Sweat gland
Thermoreceptor (hot)
Nociceptor (pain sensor)
Hair
Hair follicle
Epidermis
Dermis
Nerve
Light touch sensor
Blood vessel
Firm pressure sensor

◀ *The diagram shows a slice through human skin, with a variety of different receptors and other structures.*

The touch receptors in the skin allow us to experience the feel of different textures, such as this dog's hair.

Sensing light touch

Light touch is detected by free nerve endings in the epidermis and the outer parts of the dermis, and by sense receptors in the dermis. There are several different types of receptor for light touch. Many are clustered around root hairs. These respond when a hair is bent, allowing us to feel something as light as an insect crawling on the skin.

Sensing pressure

Touch pressure is felt when the skin is squashed out of shape, for instance, when you press with your fingertip to push a doorbell. Pressure is detected by sense receptors in the dermis. They are usually larger than the receptors for light touch, and are surrounded by a capsule. They react to tiny changes in pressure rather than to the pressure itself.

Sensing vibrations

The sense receptors that detect pressure changes also detect vibrations. Some are stimulated by slow vibrations, for example, when a textured object moves across the skin. Others are stimulated by fast vibrations, for example, when something very light moves across the skin.

Try this

Some areas of skin are more sensitive to tactile sensations than others. Mark a row of small dots on the back of your hand. Ask a friend to touch each one gently with a bristle (a stiff fiber from a brush). Without watching what your friend is doing, tell him or her when you feel the bristle. Ask your friend to record how many times you feel the bristle and how many times you do not. Then repeat the same test on the palm of your hand and on the top and bottom surfaces of your feet. Which part is most sensitive?

Other touch sensations

In addition to touch, pressure, and vibrations, we can detect itches and tickles. These, too, are tactile sensations. We are also able to detect temperature. Itches, tickles, and temperature can be detected because the skin contains sense receptors that are stimulated by them.

Sensing itches and tickles

We become aware that part of the body is itching when free nerve endings in the skin are stimulated repeatedly. The stimulation might come from a chemical such as those released by your body in response to an insect sting or bite. Rubbing the skin may relieve the itch at first, but it can actually make chemical itches worse. The scratching irritates the skin, which releases more chemicals and increases the itching.

A tickle is caused by stimulation of the same nerve endings as those involved in itching, often when something moves gently over the skin.

Sensing temperature

Temperature is detected by sense receptors called thermoreceptors. Thermoreceptors located deep in the epidermis detect cold. They are stimulated by temperatures that are lower than that of the skin. Thermoreceptors that detect heat are in the dermis and are stimulated by temperatures above

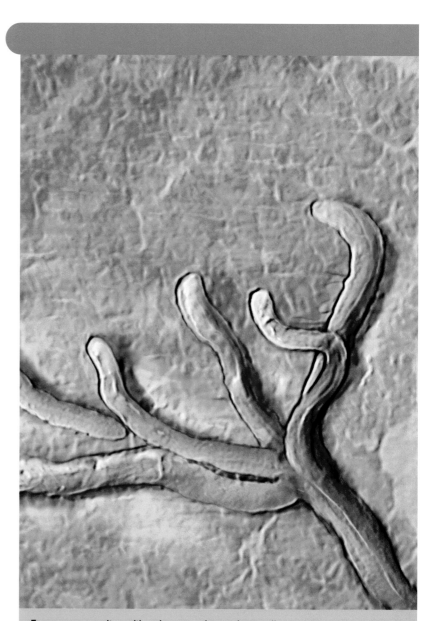

Free nerve endings like the one shown here allow us to feel light touch and other stimuli.

Try this

You can confuse your brain about the temperature of something. Prepare a bowl of cold water, one of lukewarm water, and one of hot. Put your left hand in the cold water and your right hand in the warm water for two minutes. Then put both hands into the lukewarm water at the same time.

You should find it difficult to tell how warm the water is, because it will feel hot to your left hand and cold to your right hand. Your brain will receive conflicting signals that it will find difficult to interpret.

that of the skin. A normal skin temperature is about 91.4°F (33°C).

Thermoreceptors are not spread evenly throughout the skin, but are found in clusters. Some parts of the body, such as the face, are more sensitive to heat than cold, because skin there contains more "hot" thermoreceptors than "cold" ones. There are more "cold" receptors than "hot" ones in the teeth, so teeth are much more sensitive to cold than to heat.

We can only detect the relative temperature of something, rather than its absolute temperature. This means that we can tell whether something is about as warm as our skin, or hotter or colder, but cannot tell its exact temperature in degrees.

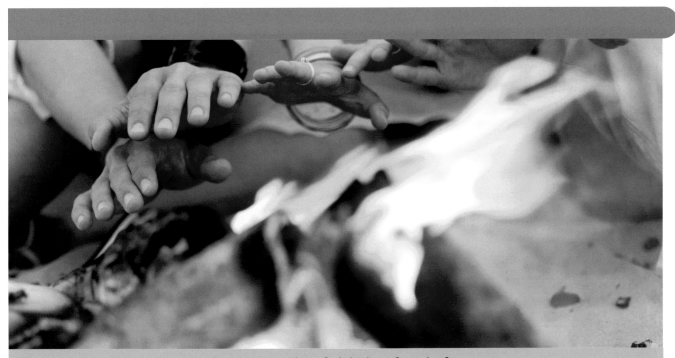

Temperature receptors in the skin allow these people to feel the heat from the fire.

Sensing pain

Most people have experienced pain at some time. Pain is usually felt when the body is injured or damaged physically or by chemicals. It can be important, alerting us to an injury that we may otherwise be unaware of.

Pain, which is detected by receptors called nociceptors, can be either fast or slow. Nociceptors are found throughout the body, with the exception of the brain itself.

Fast pain, also called sharp pain, occurs within a tiny fraction of a second of the stimulus. This is the kind of pain you feel from a needle prick. It is felt at the precise point of the stimulus.

Slow pain, also called burning or throbbing pain, develops more than a second after the stimulus and then gets stronger during the following seconds or minutes. This is the kind of pain you feel from a toothache. It is less localized than fast pain and is often felt over a wide area. Some injuries, such as banging your elbow, involve both types of pain. You feel a sharp, fast pain when you first bang it, and then slowly feel a throbbing, aching pain develop later.

Painkillers

Medicines can be taken to reduce the feeling of pain. Some, such as aspirin, ibuprofen, and acetaminophen, are called analgesics. They work by

The type of pain we get from a toothache is known as slow pain. It increases over time and can be almost unbearable.

blocking the formation of prostaglandins, which are chemicals that stimulate the nociceptors. Local anesthetics, such as Novocaine, prevent the signals from the nociceptors

reaching the brain. Some drugs, such as morphine, do not prevent pain being felt, but they change the way the brain reacts to it.

Phantom pain

A person who has had an arm or leg amputated may still "feel" tingling and pain in the missing limb. This is called phantom pain. Although it is not completely understood, doctors think it may arise when something stimulates the ends of the nerves in the remaining part of the amputated limb. Another theory is that nerve cells in the brain that were once linked to nerves in the missing limb are still active, and generate the sensation of phantom pain.

Investigate

If a doctor or dentist is going to perform a procedure that is likely to hurt the patient, they usually give the patient an anesthetic. However, anesthetics have not always been available. Find out about the history of anesthetics, and how people managed in the past.

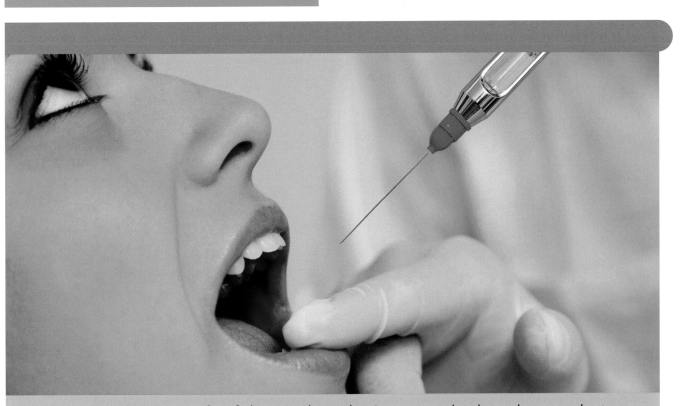

An injection of anesthetic keeps us from feeling pain when undergoing surgery, a dental procedure, or another process that would otherwise hurt.

Fun facts

Sun shades
Arctic hares have thick, black eyelashes that protect their eyes from the glare of sunlight (like a pair of sunglasses).

All eyes
Grasshoppers have five eyes.

Dog fact
Some dogs are one million times more sensitive to smells than we are.

The third eye
Tuataras are lizardlike reptiles that have a third eye on top of their heads. It is visible in hatchlings, but is covered in scales within a few months of hatching. Scientists think the eye is sensitive to ultraviolet light.

Independent eyes
The eyes of the chameleon can move independently, so it can see in two different directions at the same time.

Temperature gauge
Iguanas can detect the temperature of sand to within 2°F (1.1°C). This is important because the sand temperature is critical for the iguana to lay its eggs.

Electricity bill
Platypus have electric sensors in their bills that can detect tiny electric currents produced by other animals. Their bills also have receptors to detect touch and temperature.

Finding the way
Worker honeybees can sense magnetic fields and may use the Earth's magnetic fields for navigation.

Feeling the pressure
Butterflies have hairs on their wings to detect changes in air pressure.

Pinpointing prey
Bats can use their sense of echolocation to detect insects up to 20 feet (6 meters) away.

Night vision
Cats and some other nocturnal animals have eyes that glow in the dark. This is because they have a light-reflective layer at the back of their eyes called the tapetum. It increases the light available to the photoreceptors, which improves their vision in the dark.

The light-reflective layer at the back of this cat's eyes make them glow in the dark.

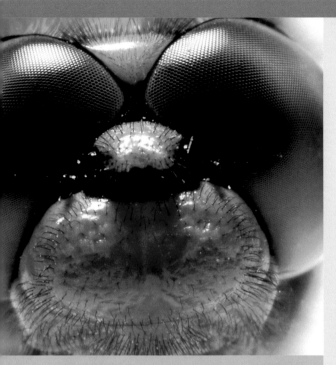

A dragonfly's compound eyes give a mosaic view of the world, made up from thousands of individual images.

Huge tongue
The giant anteater has the longest tongue in relation to its body size of any mammal.

Feel the noise
Salamanders cannot hear sounds, but some can pick up sound vibrations from the ground with their bodies.

Head in the clouds
At altitudes above 8,000 feet (2,440 meters), some mountaineers say they see strange visions and hallucinations. This is because of the lack of oxygen at these heights, which interferes with the parts of the brain involved with visual processing.

Rods and cones
The retina of a human eye contains more than 6 million cones and 110–125 million rods.

Ear protection
Ear wax is produced by sweat glands in the skin of the ear canal. It does have a useful purpose—it discourages insects from entering the ear.

Cochlea facts
The average human cochlea is about 1.25 inches (3.2 centimeters) long. It has between 16,000–20,000 hair cells and can distinguish about 1,500 separate pitches.

Sensitive hairs
Crabs have hairs on their claws and other parts of the body to detect water currents and vibrations.

Tasty worms
Earthworms have taste receptors over their whole body for sensing their surroundings.

A mosaic picture
Insects and some other creatures have compound eyes, which are made up of thousands of repeating units. They give a mosaic view of the world.

Long-distance nose
Polar bears can smell seals up to 5 miles (8 kilometers) away.

Extra eyelid
Camels have three eyelids. A clear, inner eyelid covers the eye while still letting in enough light for camels to see. The other two eyelids have extra-long eyelashes to keep sand out of the eyes.

Activities

Distortions

Look at these lines. Which are the longest and the shortest?

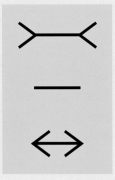

Answer: Amazingly, they are all the same length (check with a ruler if you don't believe it!). The arrowheads trick the brain into seeing the lines as different lengths.

Are the circles arranged in a straight line or are they arranged in a curve?

Answer: The tops of the circles are all in a straight line. The strong curve made by the bottom edges of the circles tricks the brain into seeing the tops in a curve, too.

Illusions

What do you see in this image?

Answer: Some people see a young girl, but others see an old witch. Sometimes, the image seems to switch back and forth between the two. It all depends on how your brain interprets the image.

Is this a white goblet or two orange faces?

Answer: As with the previous image, some people see one, some see the other, and for some people, they switch around. Again, what you see depends on how your brain interprets the image.

Which edge of the cube is closest to you?

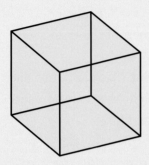

Answer: The way the cube is drawn is ambiguous. If you stare at it for a while, your brain will probably suddenly switch to a different interpretation and a different view of the cube will appear.

What shapes do you see in this diagram?

Answer: Most people see three circles, the blue outline of a triangle, and another triangle on top of it. The top triangle is not really there, the other shapes just trick your brain into imagining it.

Testing color vision

Can you see numbers in the dots?

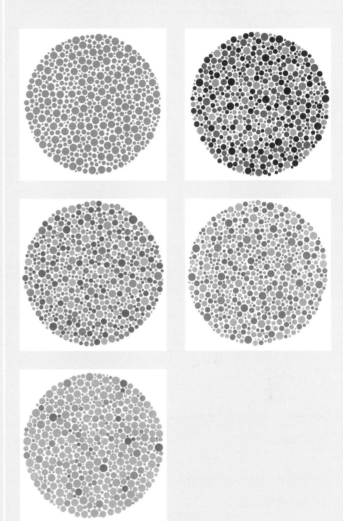

Answers: You should see the numbers 12, 42, 6, 74, and 2. If you just see a random pattern of dots, you might have a defect in your color vision and a visit to an optician might be advisable.

Glossary

Aqueous humor the watery fluid at the front of the eye

Auditory to do with the sense of hearing

Auditory tube the tube linking the middle ear with the upper part of the throat

Cilia tiny hairs

Cochlea the bony spiral in the inner ear

Cone a light-sensitive cell (photoreceptor) in the eye's retina that allows the brain to work out the color of what we are looking at

Conjunctiva the transparent layer covering the front of the eye

Cornea the transparent part of the eyeball in front of the lens

Decibel the unit used to measure the volume of sounds

Eardrum the membrane between the outer ear and middle ear

Echolocation the way in which some animals, such as bats and dolphins, use sound to locate objects in the dark

Eustachian tube alternative name for the auditory tube

Frequency the number of peaks of a wave in a given time

Hyperopia medical name for farsightedness

Iris the colored part of the eye

Laser an instrument that produces an intense beam of light that can be used in some surgical procedures

Lens the gel-like disk inside the eye

Membrane a very thin, skinlike layer

Myopia medical name for nearsightedness

Nasal cavity the space behind the nose

Nerve one of the cells along which electrical signals travel to and from the brain

Nociceptor type of sense receptor that detects pain

Olfaction the sense of smell

Olfactory to do with the sense of smell

Ossicles the three tiny bones in the middle ear

Oval window the small, membrane-covered opening between the middle ear and inner ear

Pinna the flap of skin and cartilage on the side of the head, usually called the ear

Pupil the hole at the front of the eye through which light enters the eye

Receptor a specialized cell that reacts to a stimulus such as light

Retina the light-sensitive layer at the back of the eye

Rhodopsin one of the light-sensitive chemicals of the retina

Rod a light-sensitive cell (photoreceptor) in the eye's retina that allows us to see in very dim light

Round window a small opening between the middle ear and inner ear

Sclera the white part of the eye

Semicircular canals structures in the inner ear that control balance

Sense organ a structure that responds to a stimulus

Taste bud one of the tiny structures in the tongue and other parts of the mouth that contains taste receptors

Tympanic membrane another name for the eardrum

Vestibular apparatus parts of the ear involved in controlling balance

Vitreous humor watery fluid that fills the eyeball

Wavelength the distance between the peaks of a wave

Further Information and Web Sites

Brain, Nerves, And Senses by Steve Parker (Gareth Stevens Publishing, 2004)

The Senses by A. Cassan (Chelsea Clubhouse, 2005)

What Happens When You Use Your Senses? by Jacqui Bailey (PowerKids Press, 2008)

Web Sites
Due to the changing nature of Internet links, Rosen Publishing has developed an online list of Web Sites related to the subject of this book. This site is regularly updated. Please use this link to access this list: http://www.rosenlinks.com/uhb/sens

Index